MAYER SMITH

Homeless to Heartthrob

Copyright © 2025 by Mayer Smith

All rights reserved. No part of this publication may be reproduced, stored or transmitted in any form or by any means, electronic, mechanical, photocopying, recording, scanning, or otherwise without written permission from the publisher. It is illegal to copy this book, post it to a website, or distribute it by any other means without permission.

This novel is entirely a work of fiction. The names, characters and incidents portrayed in it are the work of the author's imagination. Any resemblance to actual persons, living or dead, events or localities is entirely coincidental.

Mayer Smith asserts the moral right to be identified as the author of this work.

Mayer Smith has no responsibility for the persistence or accuracy of URLs for external or third-party Internet Websites referred to in this publication and does not guarantee that any content on such Websites is, or will remain, accurate or appropriate.

Designations used by companies to distinguish their products are often claimed as trademarks. All brand names and product names used in this book and on its cover are trade names, service marks, trademarks and registered trademarks of their respective owners. The publishers and the book are not associated with any product or vendor mentioned in this book. None of the companies referenced within the book have endorsed the book.

First edition

*This book was professionally typeset on Reedsy.
Find out more at reedsy.com*

Contents

1	The Billionaire's Challenge	1
2	Trading Luxury for Poverty	8
3	Harsh Reality	16
4	A Kind Soul	24
5	Social Worker's	32
6	Learning the Ropes	40
7	Working for Survival	47
8	Growing Connection	52
9	Character	57
10	Voiceless	62
11	The Betrayal	69
12	Billionaire Life	74
13	Heart in Two Worlds	78
14	Proving His Intentions	83
15	Grand Gesture	89
16	Scandal Exposed	95
17	Love Rekindled	102
18	New Purpose	106
19	Final Test	111
20	Happily Ever After	117

One

The Billionaire's Challenge

Nathan Sterling lounged back in the leather chair, whiskey swirling in his crystal tumbler as he smirked at the group of men seated around the dimly lit VIP lounge of The Empire Club. The scent of aged cigars and expensive cologne filled the air, mingling with the distant hum of jazz music. The conversation had taken an amusing turn—one that would change his life forever.

"You wouldn't last a week, let alone a month," scoffed Bryce Adler, a fellow billionaire heir, shaking his head with an amused chuckle.

Nathan took a slow sip of his drink, setting the glass down with deliberate ease. "You underestimate me, Bryce," he said smoothly. "Survival is all about strategy. If I had to, I could outlast any of you on the streets."

The men around the table erupted in laughter. "Oh, please," sneered Carter Montague, another of Nathan's longtime friends—if one could call their circle of privileged elites "friends." "You don't even know how much a loaf of bread costs, let alone how to survive without your trust fund cushioning every step."

Nathan leaned forward, his blue eyes gleaming with challenge. "I know how to play the game, Carter. You think because I was born rich, I wouldn't be able to adapt?"

"It's not just about adapting," said Bryce, swirling his own drink. "It's about losing everything—status, security, dignity. You wouldn't last a day sleeping on a park bench, Sterling."

Nathan's grin widened. "Then let's make it interesting."

The room quieted slightly, intrigued by his tone.

"I'll live as a homeless man for a full month," Nathan declared, setting his glass down with a satisfying clink. "No credit cards, no phone, no secret accounts. Just me, the streets, and whatever I can scrape together."

Bryce raised an eyebrow. "And what's the wager?"

Nathan leaned back again, the smugness never leaving his face. "If I succeed, each of you donates five million to the Sterling Foundation's homeless initiative."

The other men exchanged glances, considering the stakes. They all had more money than they knew what to do with, but five million wasn't pocket change, even for them.

"And if you fail?" Carter challenged.

Nathan's smirk didn't falter. "Then I match your donations, plus an extra five. Ten million from my own pocket."

The group erupted into murmurs, weighing the absurdity of the challenge.

"Deal," Bryce said finally, extending his hand.

Nathan clasped it with a firm shake, his heart pounding in his chest—not from fear, but excitement. He had always enjoyed a good gamble, and this one had high stakes written all over it.

Nathan stood in his penthouse the following evening, staring at the single duffel bag on his king-sized bed. Everything in his apartment—the Italian leather furniture, the original artwork on the walls, the grand piano in the corner—would be meaningless in the world he was about to enter.

"You're actually going through with this?" His best friend, Lucas, leaned against the doorway, arms crossed. Unlike Nathan's other rich acquaintances, Lucas had a conscience.

"Damn right I am," Nathan said, zipping the bag. "I'll be back in a month, victorious and ten million dollars richer."

"You realize this isn't some luxury retreat, right? This is real life for a lot of people."

Nathan shrugged. "I know that."

Lucas sighed. "No, you don't. But I hope you figure it out before it's too late."

Nathan ignored the warning.

He left behind his penthouse, his expensive suits, his black credit card, and his name. From now on, he was just another nameless man on the streets.

The First Night

The cold was the first thing he noticed.

Nathan stood on a busy city sidewalk as the sun set, his thin jacket doing little to keep out the chill. He had intentionally worn clothes that wouldn't give him away—an old pair of jeans, a faded hoodie, scuffed sneakers—but already, he felt the difference. People walked past him without a glance, as if he were invisible.

He had expected a challenge. He had not expected to feel… nothing.

No nods of acknowledgment. No polite smiles. Just the shuffle of hurried feet and the occasional suspicious glance from someone clutching their purse tighter.

By the time night fully set in, Nathan realized he had made his first mistake: he had nowhere to go.

The city he had ruled from glass towers and high-rise penthouses was suddenly an unwelcoming labyrinth of cold concrete. He wandered the streets, avoiding alleyways that seemed too dangerous, only to find himself in an even worse position—completely exposed.

The benches in the park were occupied by others who had already claimed their spots. Some had blankets, makeshift cardboard shelters, or at least the experience of knowing where to sleep. Nathan had none of that.

After walking for what felt like hours, his feet aching in shoes that were never meant for this kind of endurance, he spotted an empty bus stop. It wasn't much, but it was something.

Sitting down, he pulled his hood up, tucking his hands into his sleeves. The wind cut through his thin layers, biting against his skin. He had never been this cold before. Never felt hunger gnaw at him like this.

He closed his eyes, trying to ignore the hard bench beneath him.

Then he heard the footsteps.

Slow. Measured. Approaching.

Nathan's heartbeat quickened.

He kept his head down, listening.

A shadow fell over him.

"New around here?" a gruff voice asked.

Nathan looked up, meeting the sharp gaze of a man who had clearly spent years surviving these streets. His beard was unkempt, his clothes worn, but his eyes were alert—watchful.

"Yeah," Nathan said, keeping his tone casual. "Just… trying to figure things out."

The man chuckled, but there was no humor in it. "Figuring things out can get you hurt if you don't know where you belong."

Nathan tensed. He had fought in high-stakes business deals, but this was different. This was survival in its rawest form.

The man studied him a moment longer, then sighed. "If you're lucky, no one will bother you tonight. But don't count on it."

With that, he walked away, disappearing into the shadows.

Nathan exhaled, his breath visible in the night air. He leaned back against the cold metal bench, staring up at the distant skyscrapers.

For the first time in his life, he felt small.

And for the first time, he wasn't sure he would win this bet after all.

Two

Trading Luxury for Poverty

The world looked different from down here.

Nathan Sterling had spent his entire life looking down from the top—penthouse balconies, VIP booths, first-class seats—but now, seated on a grimy city bench with a threadbare hoodie pulled over his head, he saw the city from the ground up. It was colder, harsher. Unforgiving.

He hadn't slept.

The bus stop he had chosen as his resting place was far from ideal. The hard metal bench left his muscles stiff, and every passing car sent a gust of frigid air slicing through his thin jacket. Every sound—shuffling footsteps, rustling paper bags, distant shouting—kept him on edge. He had never realized how loud the city was at night.

He had tried to close his eyes, tried to block out the exhaustion gnawing at his body, but sleep never came.

Now, as the sun began to rise, casting pale gray light over the streets, Nathan felt the first true wave of regret settle in his gut.

This wasn't a game.

He could still hear Bryce's mocking voice in his head. You wouldn't last a day on the streets, Sterling.

Nathan clenched his jaw. He would prove them wrong.

But first, he needed to eat.

He had never known hunger.

Sure, he had skipped meals before—too busy closing a deal, too wrapped up in a party—but that was by choice. This was different. This was an emptiness clawing at his stomach, a dull ache that made his limbs feel weak.

Nathan reached into his pocket and pulled out the five-dollar bill he had been given at the start of this ridiculous bet. The only money he was allowed for an entire month.

He walked down the street, eyes scanning for cheap food. He passed a café but immediately ruled it out—one coffee would drain his entire budget. The scent of fresh bagels drifted from a bakery, making his stomach tighten painfully, but he knew better than to waste money on something so fleeting.

Then he saw a small, dingy convenience store on the corner.

Nathan stepped inside, the fluorescent lights buzzing overhead. The cashier, an older man with a tired face, barely glanced up.

He wandered the aisles, searching for the cheapest, most filling thing he could find. He settled on a small loaf of white bread—99 cents. A can of tuna—$1.50. A bottle of water—$1.00. That left him with just over a dollar.

As he approached the counter, he felt the cashier's eyes on him. Nathan kept his head down, suddenly aware of how different he must look. His designer jeans, once expensive, now just looked dirty. His hoodie, though once stylish, was wrinkled and unimpressive.

"That it?" the man asked, ringing up the items.

"Yeah," Nathan muttered, sliding the crumpled bill across the counter.

The man took it without a word, handing him his change and bagging the items in a thin plastic bag. Nathan turned to leave when he heard a voice behind him.

"You new out here?"

Nathan froze.

He turned slowly to find a woman watching him. She was about his age, maybe a little younger, with a messy blonde ponytail and sharp green eyes that studied him with something close to curiosity. She wore an oversized hoodie and ripped jeans, but there was a toughness to her that made it clear she had been on these streets for a while.

"I—uh—" Nathan hesitated, unsure how to answer.

The woman smirked. "Yeah. You look new. Too clean. Too awkward."

Nathan bristled. "I don't know what you're talking about."

She chuckled. "Sure you don't. But don't worry—you'll get used to it soon enough."

Then, just like that, she turned and walked away, slipping a candy bar into her pocket as she passed the counter. The cashier saw it and didn't even react.

Nathan stood there for a moment before shaking his head and stepping outside.

With his food secured, he needed to figure out his next move.

He sat on a nearby curb, pulling the loaf of bread from the bag. He tore off a piece and shoved it into his mouth, trying to ignore how dry and flavorless it was.

As he chewed, he noticed a group of men sitting a few feet away, huddled in the shade of a closed storefront. They were passing around a bottle in a paper bag, speaking in low voices.

One of them noticed him watching.

"You lost, buddy?" the man called. He was older, maybe in his late fifties, with a thick gray beard and piercing eyes.

Nathan hesitated. "No. Just… figuring things out."

The man chuckled. "That so?"

The others turned their attention to Nathan now, sizing him up.

"You got a name?" the bearded man asked.

Nathan hesitated again. Using his real name was out of the question. "Nate," he finally said.

The man nodded. "Well, Nate, you better learn the rules quick. Out here, people will take what they can. You watch your stuff, or you won't have it by morning."

Nathan swallowed hard. He hadn't considered that.

Another man, younger, probably in his thirties, smirked. "You got any cash on you, newbie?"

Nathan shook his head. "No."

The man stared at him for a long moment, then nodded slowly. "Smart answer."

Nathan tensed.

Then, to his surprise, the bearded man pulled something from his pocket and tossed it toward him.

It landed at Nathan's feet—a small granola bar.

"You'll need more than bread," the man said simply.

Nathan picked it up, staring at the wrapper. It wasn't much, but it was a gesture he hadn't expected.

"Thanks," he said cautiously.

The man just nodded and returned to his conversation.

Nathan exhaled, standing up and stuffing the granola bar into his bag. He had been out here for less than a full day, and already, he was learning that survival wasn't just about food or shelter. It was about knowing who to trust.

And more importantly—who not to.

As the evening rolled in, Nathan wandered the streets, searching for a place to sleep.

He found a quiet alley behind an old bookstore. It wasn't

perfect, but it was hidden enough to keep him out of sight. He sat down against the brick wall, pulling his hoodie tighter around him.

Just as he was about to close his eyes, he heard footsteps.

Not casual footsteps. Purposeful. Heavy.

Nathan tensed, pressing himself against the wall.

A figure appeared at the mouth of the alley—a man in a worn leather jacket, his face partially obscured by the dim light.

Nathan's pulse quickened.

"You look a little lost, kid," the man said, stepping closer.

Nathan didn't respond.

The man's eyes flicked to the plastic bag at Nathan's side. "Whatcha got in there?"

Nathan gripped the bag tighter. "Nothing."

The man smirked. "That so?"

He took another step forward.

Nathan's mind raced. He had never been in a fight before—at least, not one that wasn't handled by lawyers or security guards.

Trading Luxury for Poverty

"Look, man, I don't want any trouble," Nathan said, trying to keep his voice steady.

"Neither do I," the man replied smoothly. "But trouble tends to find people like you out here."

Nathan knew he had two choices—run or fight.

Before he could decide, a voice rang out from the street.

"Hey! Leave him alone."

The man froze, glancing over his shoulder.

Nathan followed his gaze—and saw her.

The girl from the convenience store.

Her green eyes locked onto Nathan's, filled with something between annoyance and amusement.

"Come on," she said. "I know a better place to crash."

Nathan hesitated only a second before grabbing his bag and following her.

As they disappeared into the night, he realized something.

He wasn't just playing a game anymore.

This was survival. And he had a long way to go.

Three

Harsh Reality

Nathan followed the girl through the dimly lit streets, his breath visible in the crisp night air. His heart was still pounding from the encounter in the alley. The man in the leather jacket had radiated danger—an edge Nathan wasn't used to facing without security guards or legal teams at his disposal.

Now, here he was, trailing behind a stranger, trusting that she wouldn't lead him into something worse.

"Where are we going?" he asked.

The girl glanced back, her sharp green eyes studying him. "Somewhere safer than that alley."

Nathan swallowed his skepticism and kept walking.

Harsh Reality

As they turned a corner, the city became quieter. Fewer streetlights flickered overhead, casting long shadows on the cracked pavement. It was the kind of place he'd never ventured into before, the kind of place he'd driven past without a second thought.

"You still haven't told me your name," Nathan said.

The girl smirked. "You haven't earned it yet."

Nathan frowned but didn't argue.

They stopped outside an abandoned building with boarded-up windows and graffiti covering the walls. The girl slipped through a side entrance, and Nathan hesitated before following.

Inside, the air smelled of mildew and dust. The floor was littered with old newspapers, empty cans, and broken furniture. But what caught Nathan's attention were the people—at least a dozen of them—huddled together on makeshift beds of cardboard and tattered blankets.

"This is home," the girl said, walking past a man wrapped in an old army coat. "At least, for now."

Nathan's gaze swept the room. A woman with hollow eyes rocked a child back and forth in the corner. A teenage boy stared at him from behind a pile of blankets, his expression unreadable.

He had seen reports about homelessness, read articles, even

donated to charities that helped "people like this." But he had never been in it. Never felt the weight of it.

"You can crash over there," the girl said, pointing to an empty space near the far wall. "Just don't snore. We're all light sleepers."

Nathan walked over, setting his bag down. The cold from the concrete floor seeped into his body almost immediately. He tried to get comfortable, but there was nothing comfortable about this.

"So, what's your story?" the girl asked, leaning against the wall next to him.

Nathan hesitated.

Every instinct told him to lie. To create some tragic backstory that would make sense of why a guy like him was here. But he wasn't ready to spin a tale just yet.

"Just… fell on hard times," he said finally.

The girl snorted. "Yeah, you and everyone else here."

Silence settled between them.

Nathan shifted, trying to ignore the ache in his back. "What about you?"

Her smirk faded. "Been on my own since I was sixteen. Foster care wasn't my thing. The streets are tough, but at least they're honest."

Nathan frowned. "Honest?"

She turned to look at him, and for the first time, he saw something deeper in her eyes—something tired, something knowing. "Yeah. No fake smiles. No empty promises. Out here, people show you who they really are."

Nathan didn't know what to say to that.

For the first time, he wondered if maybe she was right.

Nathan barely slept.

Every sound kept him on edge—the rustle of movement, the occasional cough, the distant sound of sirens outside. His body ached from the unforgiving floor, and his stomach twisted with hunger. The dry bread and tuna he had rationed earlier hadn't been enough.

By the time morning arrived, exhaustion weighed on him like a lead blanket.

"You get used to it," the girl said, stretching as she sat up.

Nathan wasn't sure he believed that.

People began to stir, gathering what little belongings they had.

Some left immediately, disappearing into the city, while others lingered, talking in hushed tones.

The girl stood and stretched. "You coming?"

Nathan frowned. "Where?"

"To make some money."

He hesitated.

He still had a little over a dollar left from his original five, but he knew it wouldn't last. If he wanted to eat, if he wanted to survive, he had to find a way to make more.

With a resigned sigh, he pushed himself up and followed her.

They walked for blocks, the morning air biting against Nathan's skin. The city moved around them—people rushing to work, cars honking, life continuing as if the world hadn't shifted for him.

The girl led him to a busy intersection.

"Watch and learn," she said, flashing him a grin before walking toward the stopped cars.

Nathan watched as she approached a driver, tapping on the window with a practiced ease. The man inside barely looked at her before shaking his head and rolling forward when the light turned green.

She moved to another car. This time, the driver handed her a couple of bills before speeding off.

She returned to Nathan with a triumphant smirk. "Not bad for five minutes, huh?"

Nathan crossed his arms. "You're panhandling?"

She tilted her head. "Yeah. And?"

"I—" He hesitated. He had seen people begging before, had always dismissed them with a glance. Now, standing here, he realized he was on the other side.

"You think you're too good for this?" she challenged.

Nathan clenched his jaw. "No."

"Then prove it."

She handed him a piece of cardboard and a marker.

Nathan stared at them. "You want me to—?"

She shrugged. "You wanna eat, don't you?"

Nathan looked at the people around them—men and women holding up signs, some with pets curled up at their feet, some sitting on overturned buckets.

His stomach growled.

Slowly, he took the marker and wrote the words:

Hungry. Anything helps.

Then, swallowing his pride, he walked toward the cars.

The first car ignored him.

The second driver looked at him with disgust before rolling up the window.

The third driver laughed, shaking his head before speeding off.

Nathan felt humiliation burn in his chest. He had spent his life commanding boardrooms, winning negotiations, being respected. Now, he was being looked at like trash.

"People don't like looking at what makes them uncomfortable," the girl said, standing beside him.

Nathan took a breath. He had agreed to this bet. He couldn't back down now.

An older woman in a rusted sedan pulled up and rolled down her window. "Here, sweetheart," she said, pressing a few crumpled bills into his hand. "Take care of yourself."

Nathan swallowed hard. "Thank you."

She drove off, leaving him standing there, clutching the money.

Harsh Reality

He had just begged for the first time in his life.

And someone had shown him kindness.

That night, as he sat in the abandoned building again, Nathan counted the money he had made—just under ten dollars. It wasn't much, but it was enough for food.

The girl—who still hadn't given him her name—watched him.

"You did good today," she said.

Nathan exhaled. "It felt… weird."

"Yeah." She leaned back. "But you get used to it."

Nathan wasn't sure he wanted to.

As he lay back on the hard floor, his body aching and his pride shattered, one thought kept running through his mind.

How the hell was he going to survive the next twenty-nine days?

Four

A Kind Soul

The hunger gnawed at Nathan like an animal clawing at his insides. It wasn't just the empty ache in his stomach—it was the weakness in his limbs, the lightheadedness, the way his body felt sluggish and unwilling to move.

He had spent the past two days eating only the bare minimum: a stale piece of bread, a can of tuna split in half to last longer, and the occasional granola bar that the bearded man from the shelter had tossed his way. But it wasn't enough.

It would never be enough.

He sat on the cold concrete steps of an old office building, watching the flow of pedestrians moving past him like a river that would never stop to notice a drowning man. He had never felt so invisible.

Then again, maybe it was better that way.

"You look like hell."

Nathan glanced up and saw her—the girl with the sharp green eyes and the guarded expression.

He still didn't know her name.

She leaned against the brick wall beside him, arms crossed, her hoodie pulled up against the cold. The past two nights, she had been the closest thing to an ally he had, though she never let him forget that out here, trust was dangerous.

"You eat today?" she asked.

Nathan exhaled. "Not much."

She nodded, as if she had expected that answer.

"You need real food," she said. "Come on."

Before he could argue, she was already walking away.

Nathan hesitated for only a moment before pushing himself to his feet and following.

They walked for several blocks, the city shifting around them.

The gleaming skyscrapers and high-end boutiques gave way to older, worn-down buildings, their facades cracked and weathered by time.

Nathan recognized the area. He had driven through it before, usually in the back of a chauffeured car, on his way to more important destinations. He had never paid attention to the small details—the way the people here walked with their heads down, the way the businesses looked like they were barely holding on.

Now, he was part of this world.

The girl led him to a squat, brick building with a faded sign above the door:

Hope Haven Community Center

Nathan followed her inside, the scent of warm food hitting him like a punch to the gut. His stomach twisted painfully at the smell of fresh bread, of steaming soup, of something real.

A line had formed along the side of the room, stretching toward a serving counter where volunteers handed out trays of food. The room was crowded with people of all ages—some old, some young, some with haunted eyes, others with quiet resignation.

Nathan swallowed hard.

"This place is decent," the girl said. "They don't ask too many questions, and they won't treat you like dirt."

A Kind Soul

She stepped forward, nodding toward the line. "Come on."

Nathan hesitated. "You sure it's—"

"Free? Yeah," she said, rolling her eyes. "You think most people here have money?"

Nathan bit back his pride and stepped into line.

As they moved forward, he noticed a young woman behind the counter, handing out trays with a warm smile. She had dark brown hair pulled into a ponytail and soft, intelligent eyes that held a kindness he hadn't seen in a long time.

When he reached the front of the line, she looked at him and smiled.

"Hey there," she said. "First time here?"

Nathan nodded, suddenly feeling self-conscious.

She handed him a tray with a bowl of soup, a piece of bread, and an apple. "Take your time. And if you need anything, let me know."

Nathan took the tray carefully, as if it might disappear if he wasn't careful.

"Thanks," he said, his voice quieter than he intended.

She nodded before moving on to the next person in line.

Nathan followed the girl to a table near the back of the room. They sat across from each other, and Nathan stared down at his food for a moment before finally taking a bite of the bread.

It was the best thing he had ever tasted.

He didn't realize how fast he was eating until the girl chuckled.

"Slow down, rich boy. No one's taking it from you."

Nathan paused mid-bite, shooting her a glare. "You don't know that."

She laughed, shaking her head. "Fair point."

They ate in silence for a few minutes.

Then, Nathan set his spoon down. "Who is she?"

The girl raised an eyebrow. "Who?"

"The woman behind the counter."

She followed his gaze, landing on the volunteer who had given him his tray. "Oh. That's Emily."

"She work here?"

"More like runs the place," the girl said. "She's a social worker. Helps people get back on their feet—housing, jobs, that kind of thing. She's one of the good ones."

Nathan frowned. "Why does she do it?"

The girl shrugged. "Some people just want to help."

Nathan wasn't sure he believed that.

In his world, people didn't do things out of the goodness of their hearts. There was always a motive—money, power, influence. No one gave without expecting something in return.

But as he watched Emily move from person to person, offering warm smiles and soft words of encouragement, he saw nothing but genuine kindness.

It was... strange.

As they finished eating, Emily approached their table.

"Hey," she said. "How was the food?"

"Good," the girl said. "Same as always."

Emily turned to Nathan. "You doing okay?"

Nathan hesitated. No one had asked him that since he got here.

"Yeah," he said finally. "Thanks."

Emily studied him for a moment.

"You looking for work?" she asked.

Nathan blinked. "What?"

She gestured toward the back of the room. "We need help around here. Cleaning up, organizing donations. It's not much, but we can pay a little. And you get a meal every shift."

Nathan's first instinct was to refuse.

He had never worked a day in his life. Not in the way she meant. His work had been business meetings, investment deals, high-stakes negotiations. Manual labor was something other people did.

But then he remembered his empty pockets.

His thinning supplies.

The gnawing hunger that would return by tomorrow.

And he nodded. "Yeah. I'll do it."

Emily smiled. "Great. Come by tomorrow morning, and we'll get you started."

As she walked away, Nathan felt something unexpected.

Relief.

For the first time since this bet started, he had something.

It wasn't a penthouse. It wasn't a private jet or a million-dollar deal.

But it was something.

As they left the shelter, the girl glanced at him.

"So," she said. "Guess you're sticking around, huh?"

Nathan exhaled. "For now."

She smirked. "Better get used to it."

Nathan didn't respond.

Because deep down, he knew the truth.

He wasn't just here to win a bet anymore.

He was here to survive.

Five

Social Worker's

Nathan stood outside Hope Haven Community Center as the morning chill crept into his bones. His hoodie provided little protection against the biting wind, but he had quickly learned that complaining about the cold wouldn't change a thing.

The city was already awake, bustling with people on their way to work, sipping overpriced coffee, and checking their phones. To them, he was invisible.

He clenched his fists inside his sleeves, forcing himself to take a steadying breath. Today was different. Today, he had a job—if it could even be called that.

He stepped inside the shelter, greeted by the familiar warmth and scent of food. The place was already filled with people—

some eating, some talking in hushed voices, and others simply staring into space, their faces worn with the kind of exhaustion money couldn't fix.

Emily was by the counter, organizing trays of food while speaking softly to an older woman who clutched a blanket tightly around her shoulders. The woman nodded at whatever Emily was saying before shuffling away with a tired expression.

Nathan hesitated, suddenly unsure of himself. He was used to walking into offices where people knew his name, where assistants scrambled to meet his every demand. Here, no one cared who he was. He was just another face in the crowd.

"You're late," a voice said beside him.

Nathan turned and saw Emily standing there, arms crossed, one eyebrow raised.

He frowned. "I didn't know I had a specific time to show up."

"You do now," she said, handing him a pair of work gloves. "You can start by sorting through the donation bins in the back."

Nathan looked down at the gloves, resisting the urge to scoff. Manual labor? He had expected something easier—maybe organizing files, helping with logistics, something that didn't involve digging through other people's discarded clothes.

But Emily was already walking away, clearly expecting him to follow.

Nathan sighed and did just that.

The storage room behind the main hall was cluttered with bags of donated clothes, old shoes, and random household items stacked in piles. The air smelled like fabric softener mixed with the musty scent of things that had been sitting in basements for too long.

"This is where we sort everything before it goes out to the front," Emily explained, pulling a large plastic container closer. "We separate the good from the useless. Stained, ripped, or ruined stuff gets tossed. Everything else gets folded and put out for people to take."

Nathan glanced at the piles. "And you do all this yourself?"

She shook her head. "We get volunteers, but there aren't enough hands to keep up. People donate a lot, but most of it isn't usable. You'd be surprised how many people think it's okay to donate a single shoe or a broken toaster."

Nathan smirked. "Ever get something weird?"

Emily chuckled. "Once, someone donated a wedding dress from the 80s. Puffy sleeves, pearls, the whole thing."

"Did anyone take it?"

"Yeah. A guy named Ronnie. Wore it around the shelter for two weeks straight."

Nathan let out a surprised laugh.

Emily smiled. "It made him happy, so we didn't stop him."

Nathan found himself watching her, intrigued by how easily she seemed to navigate this world. She wasn't hardened like the others. There was something resilient about her, but not in the way that suggested she had given up.

She still believed.

"Come on," she said. "Start sorting."

Nathan rolled up his sleeves, slipped on the gloves, and got to work.

At first, the task seemed simple—just clothes, right? But as Nathan sifted through the donations, he realized how much effort went into something as basic as making sure people had decent things to wear.

Some of the clothes were in terrible condition—ripped jackets, socks with holes, shirts stained beyond saving. But others were perfectly fine. He found a good pair of jeans, a thick sweater, even a winter coat that still had the tags attached.

"People donate new stuff?" he asked, holding up the coat.

"Sometimes," Emily said. "But more often than not, people dump things they don't want just to feel better about themselves."

Nathan frowned, tossing another useless shirt into the reject pile. "That's pretty messed up."

Emily shrugged. "It's how the world works. But we take what we can get."

They worked in silence for a while, the only sounds coming from the rustle of fabric and the occasional murmur of voices from the main hall.

Then Emily spoke again.

"So, what's your story?"

Nathan stiffened. "What do you mean?"

She pulled out a hoodie from the pile, inspected it, and set it aside. "You're new. And you don't look like you've been out here long. People don't just show up at places like this without a reason."

Nathan swallowed hard. He had been dreading this question.

"I just… hit a rough patch," he said vaguely.

Emily didn't press, but her eyes studied him like she saw right through the lie.

"Rough patches don't last forever," she said eventually. "You can pull yourself out."

Nathan hesitated.

Could he?

A few hours later, as they were finishing up, a commotion broke out in the main hall.

Nathan heard raised voices, followed by the sharp sound of something crashing to the floor.

Emily was already moving before he could ask what was happening.

He followed her out to the main room, where a man was yelling, his face red with anger. He was older, maybe in his sixties, his clothes worn and his beard unkempt.

"I ain't takin' no damn handout!" the man shouted.

A volunteer, a young guy in his twenties, held up his hands. "No one's saying you have to—"

"I ain't no charity case!" the man bellowed.

Emily stepped in. "Frank, calm down."

The man turned to her, his expression twisting with emotion. "I don't need your pity, Emily!"

Nathan watched, unsure what to do.

Emily didn't flinch. "No one here pities you, Frank. You're part of this place, and we take care of our own."

Frank's jaw clenched. His hands were shaking. "I—"

Emily reached out, placing a hand on his arm. "It's okay. Let's just sit down and talk, alright?"

For a moment, it seemed like Frank might explode again.

But then, his shoulders slumped, and the fight drained out of him.

Emily guided him to a chair, sitting with him as he rubbed his hands over his face.

Nathan exhaled, tension slowly leaving his body.

He had no idea how she did it.

As the day wound down, Nathan found himself sitting outside the shelter, staring at the skyline in the distance.

Emily joined him, handing him a bottle of water.

"You did good today," she said.

Nathan let out a breath. "I barely did anything."

"You worked. That's more than most people who come through here."

Nathan didn't know what to say.

After a moment, Emily stood. "You coming back tomorrow?"

He hesitated.

Then, to his own surprise, he nodded. "Yeah."

Emily smiled. "Good."

As she walked back inside, Nathan sat there, staring at the place he had once ignored.

For the first time, he wondered if maybe, just maybe, this was exactly where he was supposed to be.

Six

Learning the Ropes

The next morning, Nathan arrived at Hope Haven before the sun had fully risen. The streets were still quiet, the city's usual noise replaced by the occasional hiss of a passing bus or the shuffle of someone's footsteps. He hadn't told Emily he'd come this early, but his restlessness had driven him out of his makeshift bed and back to the one place that seemed to hold any sense of purpose.

When he stepped inside, he was greeted by the familiar hum of fluorescent lights and the faint scent of coffee. Volunteers were already at work, sorting donated clothes, arranging food supplies, and setting up tables for the day's visitors. Emily was in the corner with a clipboard, her brow furrowed as she read through a list. She glanced up when she saw him.

"Couldn't wait to get back to work?" she asked, a hint of

amusement in her tone.

"Something like that," Nathan said, his hands in his pockets.

Emily tilted her head toward the storage area. "Good. We've got plenty to do."

Nathan followed her back, readying himself for another day of sorting clothes. But instead of bins of fabric, Emily stopped beside a stack of boxes filled with canned goods and dry pasta.

"Today, you're helping with the food pantry," she said.

Nathan blinked. "The food pantry?"

"Yep. We hand out groceries once a week to families who can't make it to the soup kitchen or prefer to cook at home. You'll be packing bags, restocking shelves, and keeping track of what we have left."

He nodded, unsure if he was relieved or nervous about the new responsibility. Sorting clothes had been mindless work. This sounded more… involved.

Emily handed him a clipboard with a list of items that needed to go into each bag. She walked him through the shelves, showing him where everything was stored, and how to keep track of inventory. Nathan listened carefully, his mind focused on getting the details right.

As the morning passed, more people began to arrive. Some

were volunteers, others were families who lined up at the front desk to receive their weekly rations. Nathan worked steadily, packing bags and marking off items on his list. He was surprised by how quickly the shelves emptied. It was one thing to hear statistics about food insecurity on the news; it was another to see the reality of it, box by box.

Halfway through the shift, a woman approached him with a small child in tow. Her face was lined with exhaustion, her clothes faded and worn.

"Excuse me," she said softly. "Do you have any diapers left?"

Nathan checked the shelves, his stomach sinking when he saw they were completely out. He turned back to her. "I'm sorry, we just ran out. But we should have more by next week."

Her shoulders slumped, and she nodded. "Okay. Thanks anyway."

Nathan watched her leave, the child clutching her hand. He felt a pang of guilt, even though he knew it wasn't his fault.

As the day went on, he encountered more of the same. Families grateful for whatever they could get, but always needing more than what was available. It was draining, both physically and emotionally.

By the time the last family had been served, Nathan was exhausted. His arms ached from lifting boxes, and his mind was heavy with the weight of what he had seen. He sat down on a stool near the shelves, running a hand through his hair.

Emily appeared a moment later, a cup of water in her hand. "You survived," she said, offering it to him.

He took it gratefully, drinking deeply before replying. "Barely."

Emily smiled. "You did good. It's not easy seeing people struggle, but you kept going."

Nathan didn't know how to respond. He wasn't sure he deserved any praise. All he had done was follow instructions, pack bags, and tell people they were out of what they needed. It felt like he had barely scratched the surface of helping anyone.

As they finished cleaning up, Emily glanced at him. "We could use someone like you here more often. You've got a good head on your shoulders."

Nathan raised an eyebrow. "I've been here two days. That's enough to convince you?"

Emily shrugged. "I can tell when someone's got potential. And you—"

She stopped mid-sentence, her expression shifting to something more serious. She turned her head slightly, listening.

Nathan frowned. "What is it?"

"Do you hear that?" she asked, her voice low.

He listened closely, the faint sound of shuffling footsteps coming from the storage room. Emily set down her clipboard, motioning for Nathan to follow her.

They moved quietly toward the back, the dim lighting casting long shadows across the walls. The sound grew louder—something scraping against the floor.

Emily reached the doorway first, peering inside. She froze.

"What is it?" Nathan whispered.

Emily put a finger to her lips, signaling for him to stay back. She stepped inside, her movements cautious but steady.

Nathan's pulse quickened. He didn't know what she had seen, but the tension in the air was palpable. He stayed just outside the doorway, straining to hear.

Then came a voice—a man's voice, low and gruff.

"I didn't take nothin', I swear."

Emily's voice followed, calm and steady. "It's okay. No one's accusing you of anything. But you can't be back here alone. This area is for staff only."

Nathan stepped forward just enough to see inside. A man was crouched near one of the shelves, his clothes tattered and his face gaunt. He held a can of soup in one hand, his fingers trembling.

Learning the Ropes

Emily was standing a few feet away, her hands open at her sides, a non-threatening gesture.

"I just needed somethin' to eat," the man said, his voice cracking. "I wasn't tryin' to steal."

"We understand," Emily said gently. "But you have to come to the front. We'll get you what you need. You don't have to hide back here."

Nathan's heart pounded as he watched. The man looked desperate, like a cornered animal unsure whether to fight or flee.

Emily took a slow step closer. "You're not in trouble. Just come with me, and we'll get you some food. Okay?"

The man hesitated, his gaze darting between Emily and Nathan. Then, slowly, he set the can down and stood.

Emily smiled, the tension easing from her posture. "Thank you. Let's get you taken care of."

She led the man back toward the main hall, leaving Nathan standing there in the quiet storage room.

He exhaled a shaky breath, realizing how tightly he'd been gripping the edge of the doorframe.

When Emily returned, she gave him a reassuring look. "It happens sometimes. People get desperate."

Nathan nodded, his mind racing.

He had thought he knew what desperation looked like. He had seen it in corporate negotiations, in high-stakes deals, in the eyes of competitors who would do anything to win.

But this was different.

This was survival.

Seven

Working for Survival

The days began to blur together, each one dragging Nathan deeper into the unfamiliar rhythms of street life. His hands grew calloused from the repetitive tasks at the shelter: stacking food, sorting clothing, sweeping floors. He moved through these duties with a quiet determination, channeling his frustration and hunger into the simple work that allowed him, for a few precious hours each day, to feel human again.

The weather worsened. Rain fell relentlessly for two days straight, soaking through his thin jacket and sneakers. The shelter was crowded during the storms, filled with damp bodies and the smell of wet clothes. Nathan took refuge near a corner, keeping his head down as he listened to the steady patter of rain on the roof. His muscles ached from sleeping on concrete, but he didn't complain. There was no one to complain to, and even if there had been, he wouldn't have wasted his breath.

In the evenings, when Emily was around, she would occasionally check in on him. She never asked too many questions, never pried. It was as though she knew he wasn't ready to share his story, and in some ways, Nathan was grateful for that. He didn't want her to know who he really was, not yet. He wasn't ready to face the judgment or the questions that would inevitably come.

But he couldn't ignore the gnawing thought in the back of his mind: he was running out of time.

The bet loomed over him like a dark cloud. Nathan had agreed to spend a month living on the streets, surviving without his wealth, but the days were ticking by faster than he'd expected. He had no way of keeping track of how long he'd been out here—no phone, no watch, no sense of time beyond the rising and setting of the sun. He only knew that each day brought him closer to the end, and he had nothing to show for it.

He had learned to hustle in his own way, doing small jobs here and there. He swept floors at a nearby convenience store in exchange for a sandwich. He carried boxes for a delivery driver who couldn't be bothered to unload them alone. It wasn't much, but it was enough to keep him from starving. And it taught him something he'd never truly understood before: the value of each dollar.

One morning, as Nathan stood in line at the soup kitchen, he overheard a conversation between two older men. They spoke

Working for Survival

in low voices, their words blending into the murmur of the crowd. But one sentence caught his attention.

"There's a guy over on East 14th who'll pay twenty bucks for a day's work," the man on the left said.

Nathan turned slightly, pretending not to listen.

"Yeah?" the other man replied. "What kind of work?"

"Moving furniture. He's got a bunch of old stuff in a storage unit he needs to clear out."

Nathan didn't hear the rest of the conversation, but that one phrase stuck with him. Twenty bucks for a day's work. It wasn't much, but it was more than he'd made in a week.

He decided to find the man on East 14th.

The next morning, after his shift at the shelter, Nathan set out. The address wasn't hard to find—a run-down storage facility on the edge of the city. The place looked abandoned, the metal doors covered in rust and graffiti. Nathan hesitated, wondering if he'd been tricked, but then he saw a man standing outside, smoking a cigarette.

"Looking for work?" the man asked, his voice gruff.

Nathan nodded.

"Got a bunch of old furniture in there," the man said, gesturing to one of the units. "I need it moved out and loaded onto a truck. You up for it?"

"Yeah," Nathan replied.

The man sized him up, then nodded. "Alright. Twenty bucks when the job's done."

Nathan spent the next six hours hauling heavy dressers, sagging couches, and stacks of boxes. His arms burned, his back ached, and sweat soaked through his shirt despite the cool weather. The work was grueling, but he kept his head down and pushed through.

When the last piece of furniture was loaded onto the truck, the man handed him a crumpled twenty-dollar bill.

"Good work," he said before driving off.

Nathan stared at the bill in his hand, the edges worn and the ink faded. It was more than just money—it was proof that he could survive without his wealth, without his name. It was a small victory, but it felt monumental.

He tucked the bill into his pocket and walked back to the shelter, his body sore but his spirits higher than they'd been in weeks. He was learning how to navigate this life, how to scrape by with whatever he could find.

That night, as he sat in the corner of the shelter, Nathan caught Emily watching him. She didn't say anything, just offered him a small smile before turning back to her clipboard.

For the first time, he felt like he might actually make it through the month.

Eight

Growing Connection

It had been nearly three weeks since Nathan first set foot in the shelter. The days had grown shorter, the nights colder, and the challenges more relentless. Despite everything, he felt a subtle shift within himself. Each morning as he walked through the doors of Hope Haven, he felt less like an outsider and more like a part of something—something real.

The relationship between him and Emily had developed slowly, almost imperceptibly. She continued to treat him with the same kindness she showed to everyone else who walked through the shelter's doors. But there was a difference in how she spoke to him now, a softness that hinted at a growing trust. Nathan found himself looking forward to their conversations, even if they were brief.

He caught himself lingering when she stopped to chat, asking questions about the shelter, the people, the way everything worked. She always answered with patience, her voice carrying a warmth that cut through the cold of the city streets. Emily's dedication fascinated him, and before he realized it, he was seeking her out whenever he had a free moment.

One afternoon, as Nathan finished sorting through a pile of donated winter coats, Emily walked over, her arms folded and a thoughtful expression on her face.

"You're getting good at that," she said.

Nathan smirked. "Practice makes perfect, right?"

She smiled, but there was something more serious behind her eyes. "You've been here a while now. You must have noticed... it's not just about handing out food or sorting clothes. There's more to it than that."

Nathan paused. "What do you mean?"

Emily pulled up a folding chair and sat down, motioning for him to do the same. She leaned forward slightly, her hands clasped together.

"People come here because they have nowhere else to go," she said, her voice low and measured. "But the hardest part isn't just meeting their basic needs. It's helping them believe they can get back on their feet. That they have value. That they're not invisible."

Nathan shifted in his seat, unsure how to respond. He'd always been taught that success came from strategy, from control, from outsmarting the competition. But here, none of those tactics applied. The people who came to Hope Haven weren't competitors; they were survivors. And Emily seemed to understand that in a way he couldn't yet grasp.

"I see it in you," she continued. "You've got more to offer than you think. You've been here long enough to see how this place works, and I can tell you're starting to get it."

Nathan felt a strange mixture of pride and discomfort. "I'm just… doing what needs to be done."

"That's what we all do," Emily said, her lips curving into a faint smile. "But it matters. More than you realize."

As she stood, she placed a hand on his shoulder. "You're doing good work, Nathan. Keep it up."

Her touch was brief, but it left him feeling unexpectedly grounded. For a man who had spent his life surrounded by wealth, power, and people who only cared about what they could get from him, Emily's words carried a weight he wasn't prepared for.

Nathan watched her walk away, his mind churning.

In the days that followed, he found himself noticing things he hadn't paid attention to before. The way people's faces lit up when Emily spoke to them. The way she remembered everyone's names, their stories, their needs. The way she fought—quietly, but fiercely—for the shelter to remain a safe haven in a city that often turned a blind eye.

One evening, as they locked up the shelter together, Nathan worked up the nerve to ask a question that had been gnawing at him for days.

"Why do you do it?"

Emily stopped, her key hovering over the lock. "Do what?"

"All of this," he said, gesturing around. "You could have chosen an easier career. Something less… overwhelming."

She looked at him for a long moment, as if weighing how much to say. Finally, she leaned against the doorframe, her expression softening.

"Because it matters," she said. "Because I've seen what happens when people are left to fend for themselves. And because I know how it feels to have no one to turn to."

Nathan studied her face, searching for a trace of the pain behind her words. She didn't elaborate, and he didn't press. But he understood, at least a little.

"Do you ever feel like it's too much?" he asked.

"Every day," she admitted. "But I'd rather face the struggle than do nothing. If I can make a difference for even one person, then it's worth it."

Nathan nodded slowly, his respect for her deepening. In that moment, he saw Emily not just as a kind-hearted social worker, but as someone who carried the weight of other people's burdens because she believed in something greater than herself.

And for the first time in his life, Nathan felt a pang of something he couldn't quite name—admiration, perhaps. Maybe even something more.

As they parted ways that night, Nathan couldn't shake the feeling that Emily had started to see him differently too. She still didn't know the truth about who he was, but she saw something in him that he hadn't seen in himself for a long time: potential.

Nathan lay awake that night, staring up at the ceiling of the shelter. The city was quiet, the hum of distant traffic barely audible.

He thought about Emily's words, her conviction, and the way she had looked at him as if he were capable of something more.

And for the first time since this bet began, Nathan wondered if he could be.

Nine

Character

Nathan wiped the sweat from his brow and leaned against the broom handle, his body aching after a full day of cleaning the shelter's main hall. The floor gleamed now, the scent of disinfectant lingering in the air. Emily had already left for the evening, trusting him and a few others to finish up. He glanced around the quiet room, the usual bustling energy replaced by stillness.

He didn't mind the silence. It gave him a chance to think.

A month ago, his life had been filled with the hum of luxury—glittering parties, high-stakes business deals, and constant distraction. Now, the world had narrowed to a few simple tasks: sweeping floors, sorting donations, serving meals. But as monotonous as it seemed, each action carried weight. Every broom stroke, every meal served, every smile given or received—it all mattered in a way he had never understood before.

Nathan looked up as the front door creaked open, letting in a blast of cool night air. He tensed automatically, unsure who would be coming in this late. A figure stepped into the doorway, silhouetted against the streetlight.

"Nate?" a voice called.

His stomach dropped.

It was Bryce.

Nathan froze, his grip tightening on the broom. Bryce Adler, his long-time friend and one of the wealthiest men in the city, stood there in his tailored coat and polished shoes, looking completely out of place in the humble shelter.

"Man, I knew I'd find you here," Bryce said, stepping further inside. His sharp blue eyes darted around, taking in the tables, the racks of clothing, the kitchen in the back. "Wow. This is where you've been hiding?"

Nathan's heart pounded. He had no idea how Bryce had found him, but the sight of his old friend here was jarring. Bryce represented everything Nathan had left behind, everything he was trying to prove he didn't need.

"What are you doing here?" Nathan asked, his voice low.

Character

Bryce smirked, strolling up to him. "What do you think? I came to check on you. Thought maybe you'd have quit by now."

Nathan set the broom aside, crossing his arms. "Well, I didn't."

Bryce laughed, the sound echoing in the empty room. "I have to say, I'm impressed. You've been slumming it for weeks now. Honestly, I didn't think you'd last."

Nathan narrowed his eyes. "If you're just here to gloat—"

"Relax," Bryce interrupted, holding up a hand. "I'm not gloating. I'm genuinely curious. How are you even surviving out here?"

Nathan hesitated. "I work. I eat. I do what I need to do."

"Yeah, but why?" Bryce tilted his head. "You've got nothing to prove. It's a stupid bet. You don't have to suffer like this."

Nathan felt a flash of anger. "You don't get it, do you?"

Bryce raised an eyebrow. "Get what?"

"That it's not about proving something to you or Carter or anyone else. It's about—" Nathan stopped himself. He wasn't sure he could put it into words.

Bryce waited, his expression curious. When Nathan didn't continue, he chuckled and reached into his coat pocket. He pulled out a sleek, black credit card and held it up.

"Here," Bryce said. "Take this. Go buy yourself a decent meal, a hotel room. Get back to your life."

Nathan stared at the card. His first instinct was to grab it, to let it all be over. But then he thought of Emily, of the people he had met at the shelter, of the stories he had heard. He thought of the woman who came in every week looking for diapers, of the man who had broken down crying when someone finally listened to him.

And he thought of himself—the person he had become in the weeks since he started this journey.

"No," Nathan said quietly.

Bryce blinked. "What?"

"No," Nathan repeated, more firmly. "I'm not taking it."

Bryce frowned. "You're serious?"

Nathan nodded.

For a moment, neither of them spoke. Then Bryce let out a slow breath and slipped the card back into his pocket.

"Okay," Bryce said, his tone unreadable. "Okay, Nate. I get it. You're serious about this."

Nathan didn't respond.

Bryce took a step back, studying him. "You know, you've changed. You're not the same guy I made that bet with."

Nathan shrugged. "Maybe that's a good thing."

Bryce looked at him for another long moment before nodding. "Maybe it is."

Without another word, Bryce turned and walked out, the door swinging shut behind him.

Nathan stood there, his heart still racing, his mind a whirlwind of emotions. He had faced temptation, faced the easy way out, and he had said no. It was a small victory, but it felt enormous.

He picked up the broom and returned to his work.

Ten

Voiceless

～◦◦◦～

Nathan woke to a sharp knock on the shelter's office door, the sound cutting through the quiet like an alarm. He sat up, rubbing the sleep from his eyes. He hadn't meant to doze off in the back room again, but the relentless schedule and constant activity had left him with little energy.

Another knock, louder this time. He got up and opened the door. Standing there was Mr. Caldwell, the building's landlord. His sharp suit and colder expression immediately set Nathan on edge. Caldwell rarely came around, and when he did, it was never good news.

"We need to talk," Caldwell said curtly, stepping past Nathan into the office without waiting for an invitation.

Nathan closed the door and turned to face him. "What's this about?"

Caldwell's eyes flicked over the cluttered desk, the stacks of paperwork and donation forms that Emily had been sorting. "I'll keep it simple," he said. "You're out of time. This place needs to be cleared out by the end of the month."

Nathan's stomach dropped. "What? That can't be right. I thought we had more time—"

"You had more time," Caldwell interrupted. "But that was before certain 'community leaders' decided they could make better use of the property."

Nathan's mind raced. He'd heard Emily mention some zoning disputes before, some legal hoops she was jumping through to keep Hope Haven running. But it always seemed like she had it under control.

"Emily didn't say anything about this," Nathan said, his voice tinged with unease.

Caldwell smirked. "She probably hoped it would blow over. But it hasn't. The eviction notice is final. I suggest you start packing."

Before Nathan could respond, Caldwell brushed past him and walked out, his expensive cologne lingering in the air.

Nathan stood in the small office, his heart pounding. The

shelter was more than just a building. It was a lifeline for countless people who had nowhere else to go. If it closed, what would happen to them?

What would happen to him?

—-

Nathan found Emily in the main hall, setting up tables for the lunch rush. Her usual calm demeanor was replaced by a strained expression, the corners of her mouth tight as she moved from one table to the next.

"Emily," Nathan called, hurrying over to her.

She glanced up, her face lighting up briefly before she saw the look on his. "What is it?"

"Caldwell was just here," Nathan said, lowering his voice. "He says we're out of time. He's kicking us out."

Emily froze, her hands gripping the edge of a table. "He told you that?"

Nathan nodded. "Why didn't you say anything?"

She exhaled, the tension in her shoulders visible. "I didn't want to worry everyone. I thought I had more time to sort things out."

"What can we do?" Nathan asked.

Emily straightened, her jaw set. "I'm not giving up without a fight. I've got a lawyer working on an injunction. If we can stall the eviction, maybe we can figure out a way to save the shelter."

"Do you think it'll work?"

"I don't know," Emily admitted. "But I have to try."

Nathan studied her face, her determination unwavering despite the looming threat. He felt a surge of respect for her—she wasn't just running a shelter; she was fighting for the lives of everyone who relied on it.

"I'll help," Nathan said firmly.

Emily looked at him, her eyes softening. "Thank you. I could use all the help I can get."

—-

The next few days were a blur of phone calls, meetings, and late-night strategy sessions. Emily juggled her usual responsibilities while trying to navigate the legal red tape. Nathan pitched in wherever he could, running errands, gathering signatures for petitions, and rallying the shelter's residents to speak out against the closure.

But the closer the deadline came, the more it felt like they were running out of options. Caldwell's threats loomed large, and each day brought more bad news. The city council had denied their initial appeal. The zoning board refused to reconsider their decision. The lawyer's injunction was delayed.

One evening, as Nathan and Emily sat in the office going over a mountain of paperwork, Nathan finally spoke what had been on his mind.

"What if it's not enough?" he asked, his voice heavy.

Emily didn't answer right away. She stared at the stack of documents, her fingers tracing the edges of a petition. "It has to be," she said quietly. "Because if we fail, these people lose everything. And I can't let that happen."

Her words hung in the air, a quiet vow that Nathan felt in his chest.

—-

The day of the final hearing arrived, a cold and cloudy morning that matched the mood of the shelter. Nathan stood outside the courthouse with Emily, their lawyer, and a small group of shelter residents who had come to show their support.

The proceedings were tense, the arguments back and forth draining what little hope they had left. Caldwell's lawyers were relentless, painting the shelter as a drain on the community, a liability that needed to be removed.

Emily's lawyer fought back, pointing out the vital services the shelter provided, the lives it had saved, the futures it had helped rebuild. Nathan watched Emily as she sat beside the lawyer, her hands clasped tightly together, her knuckles white.

When the judge finally delivered the verdict, it felt like the air was sucked out of the room. The injunction was denied. The eviction order stood.

Emily stood slowly, her face pale but composed. "Thank you, Your Honor," she said, her voice steady despite the crushing weight of the decision.

Nathan followed her out of the courthouse, unsure of what to say.

"Emily—" he began.

"We're not done," she said, cutting him off. "There's still time before the eviction takes effect. I'll keep fighting."

Nathan looked at her, marveling at her resolve. "How can you keep going after that?"

"Because I have to," Emily said simply. "If I give up, what happens to everyone who depends on us? If I stop fighting, then they lose their last hope."

Nathan felt a lump form in his throat. He had come into this world on a bet, but now it wasn't just about proving something to Bryce or anyone else. It was about standing beside Emily, about defending the people who had become more than just faces in a crowd.

"We'll figure it out," he said, his voice firm.

Emily met his eyes, and for a moment, he saw something in her expression that gave him hope.

"Thank you," she said softly. "I'm glad you're here."

Nathan nodded, a new determination taking root. They had lost the battle, but the war wasn't over. Not yet.

Eleven

The Betrayal

Nathan paced the length of the shelter's empty main hall, the echoes of his footsteps bouncing off the walls. The place had been quieter than usual since the court's decision. Most of the residents were still coming in and out, but the looming eviction had cast a shadow over everything. Even Emily's usually reassuring presence felt strained. She spent most of her time in the office now, pouring over legal documents, making desperate phone calls, and trying to rally support from anyone who would listen.

Nathan had done everything he could to help. He'd made calls, written emails, even stood on street corners collecting signatures for a last-ditch petition. But the weight of the deadline pressed down harder with each passing day, and the closer it got, the more it felt like a noose tightening around the shelter.

He stopped pacing and leaned against one of the tables, his arms crossed as he stared at the floor. He had to admit, a part of him felt defeated. He had started this whole ordeal as a cocky billionaire, confident he could endure a month of hardship for the sake of a bet. But now... now it wasn't about the bet anymore. He didn't even care if he "won" or not. This was about something bigger—about the people who had taken him in when he had nothing, the people who depended on this place to survive.

The sound of the front door opening snapped Nathan out of his thoughts. He turned, expecting to see one of the usual volunteers, but instead, he was greeted by the last person he wanted to see: Carter.

Carter Montague strode into the shelter like he owned it, his expensive coat and leather shoes glaringly out of place against the worn linoleum floor and folding chairs. He looked around with an air of disdain, his expression a mix of amusement and disbelief.

"Well, well," Carter drawled. "Look at you, Nathan. Playing the noble pauper. I almost didn't believe it when Bryce told me, but here you are."

Nathan straightened, his jaw tightening. "What are you doing here, Carter?"

Carter grinned, his perfect teeth flashing. "Checking on an old friend. Seeing how he's doing in his new... circumstances."

The Betrayal

Nathan crossed his arms. "I don't need you to check on me."

"No?" Carter walked further into the room, his gaze lingering on the donation bins and the rows of folding tables. "Because it looks like you're in over your head. Bryce said you were serious about this, but I thought for sure you'd have bailed by now. Yet here you are, still pretending to be one of them."

"I'm not pretending," Nathan said sharply.

Carter smirked. "Sure you're not. But let's be honest—how long are you planning to keep this charade up? A few more days? A week? And then what? You go back to your penthouse, your board meetings, your private jets. You get to pat yourself on the back and say you lived like a 'normal' person for a month. Then it's back to business as usual."

Nathan felt a surge of anger. "It's not like that."

"No?" Carter raised an eyebrow. "So you're planning to stay here forever, is that it? Or maybe you've found your calling as a charity worker."

Nathan clenched his fists. "What I do isn't any of your business."

Carter laughed. "Come on, Nathan. Don't kid yourself. This isn't who you are. You're not one of them. You're just... slumming it for a while. Playing a part. But in the end, you'll go back to the life you always had, and they'll still be here. Nothing's going to change."

Nathan's jaw tightened, his anger boiling just beneath the surface. He had thought the same thing once, back when he first arrived. He had assumed this place would be just a stop on a journey that would eventually lead him back to his old life. But now, after weeks of living it, after seeing what people like Emily did every day, after hearing the stories of the people who relied on the shelter, he couldn't dismiss it so easily.

"What do you want, Carter?" Nathan asked, his voice cold.

Carter tilted his head. "I want you to come back to reality. This bet of yours—this little social experiment—it's gone on long enough. You've proven your point, whatever that point was. Bryce and I have already moved on. You should too."

Nathan shook his head. "I'm not leaving."

Carter's grin faltered, his expression hardening. "You're serious?"

Nathan met his gaze. "I'm staying."

Carter stared at him for a long moment, then laughed quietly. "Wow. You've actually bought into it. I didn't think you had it in you."

Nathan didn't reply.

"Well," Carter said, slipping his hands into his coat pockets, "if that's how you want to play it, fine. But just remember: when this place gets shut down, when everyone here is back out on

The Betrayal

the street, you'll be able to walk away. They won't. And you'll have to live with that."

He turned and walked toward the door, his footsteps echoing in the empty hall. Nathan watched him go, his chest tight, his mind racing. Carter's words cut deeper than he wanted to admit. Was he right? Was Nathan just playing a part, trying to prove something to himself and his old friends? Or was there more to it now?

As the door closed behind Carter, Nathan sat down heavily on one of the folding chairs. He stared at the floor, his thoughts a tangled mess. He had come here to win a bet, but somewhere along the way, it had become more than that. He had started to care—about the people, about the shelter, about Emily. He didn't want to walk away, but he didn't know if he could stop what was coming.

Carter's visit had shaken him, but it had also steeled his resolve. Whatever happened next, Nathan knew one thing for sure: he wasn't going to give up without a fight.

Twelve

Billionaire Life

Nathan stood in front of the elevator doors on the top floor of Sterling Tower, his reflection sharp and unrecognizable in the mirrored surface. His old life, the one he'd left behind when he'd accepted the bet, came rushing back with every step he took into his family's corporate headquarters. The quiet hum of the building, the faint scent of polished wood and fresh coffee, even the subtle pressure of the perfectly tailored suit he now wore—it all felt foreign, like slipping into someone else's skin.

He glanced down at his phone, seeing a flurry of unread messages. His assistant, Rebecca, had been working overtime to reschedule meetings, apologize for his unexplained absence, and piece together the shattered image of Nathan Sterling, the billionaire playboy. She had been tactful—she always was—but her messages were edged with a concern that hadn't been there before. She wanted to know what had changed.

Nathan wasn't sure how to answer.

When the elevator doors slid open, a familiar voice greeted him.

"Nathan!" Bryce's smooth, polished tone carried over the quiet murmur of the office.

Nathan turned to see Bryce and Carter standing near the expansive glass windows that overlooked the city. Both men were immaculately dressed, their appearances and confidence unshaken, as though the bet had been nothing more than a passing joke. Bryce held a glass of scotch, the ice clinking softly as he approached.

"Back from your little... adventure, I see," Bryce said, a smile tugging at the corner of his mouth. "How was it? Enlightening?"

Nathan forced a polite smile and stepped out of the elevator. "Something like that."

Carter laughed, his arms crossed over his chest. "I'm impressed you actually stuck it out. Honestly, I didn't think you'd last more than a week."

"I told you I would," Nathan said, his voice even.

"And now you're back," Bryce said, his grin widening. "Back where you belong. Time to put all that behind you, right?"

Nathan hesitated. He glanced out the window at the city below, the skyline glittering in the early evening light. The shelter wasn't far from here. He could still picture the faces of the people he'd met, the stories he'd heard. The memory of Emily's unwavering determination felt like a weight in his chest.

"I'm not sure it's that simple," Nathan said finally.

Bryce raised an eyebrow. "Oh? Why not?"

"I learned a lot," Nathan said carefully. "More than I expected. It wasn't just about surviving out there. It was about understanding—about seeing what I'd been blind to before."

Carter snorted. "Let me guess. You found meaning in the struggle? You discovered the value of a simpler life? Come on, Nathan. Don't tell me you've turned into one of those idealists."

Nathan clenched his jaw but didn't rise to the bait. Instead, he turned back to Bryce. "It's not about idealism. It's about responsibility. We've been so focused on what we can get, we've never thought about what we can give. And now, I can't ignore it. I can't go back to pretending it doesn't exist."

Bryce's smile faltered. "You're serious."

"I am."

Carter shook his head, chuckling. "Unbelievable. You go off the grid for a month, and suddenly you think you're some kind of saint. Look, Nathan, I'm glad you won the bet—really, I am. But let's not get carried away. You're a businessman, not a philanthropist."

"Maybe I can be both," Nathan shot back.

Bryce exchanged a glance with Carter, and for a moment, the room was heavy with tension. Then Bryce sighed and clapped a hand on Nathan's shoulder.

"Well," Bryce said, "if anyone can pull it off, it's you."

Carter rolled his eyes. "I give it two weeks."

Nathan ignored him. He turned to the windows again, his gaze distant.

Two weeks ago, he would have laughed off Carter's words, would have gone straight to the private lounge for a drink and a recap of his so-called adventure. But now, as he stood here, surrounded by the trappings of his old life, he felt a deep sense of unease. The bet had changed him in ways he was only beginning to understand.

And he wasn't sure if he would ever be the same again.

Thirteen

Heart in Two Worlds

Nathan stood at the edge of the rooftop garden atop Sterling Tower, his hands gripping the metal railing as he stared out at the city skyline. The sun dipped low, casting golden light over the sprawling metropolis, its towers gleaming like beacons of wealth and ambition. From this height, the world seemed distant, untouchable. But for the first time in his life, Nathan felt disconnected from the very city he had once ruled.

It had been a week since his return to the life he had temporarily abandoned. A week filled with long meetings, eager assistants, and a packed schedule designed to reinsert him into the elite world he'd always known. On paper, things were back to normal. His businesses were running smoothly, his public image was intact, and his absence was written off as a personal retreat to "gain fresh perspective."

But it wasn't normal. Not to him.

He closed his eyes, and his mind wandered back to Hope Haven. He could still hear Emily's voice, calm and steady, as she guided people through the shelter's small but vital operations. He could still see the lined faces of the residents, their weary eyes, their quiet gratitude. He thought of the child clinging to her mother, the elderly man who had offered Nathan a piece of bread from his own meager stash, and the quiet moments he'd spent folding donated clothes in the back room.

It wasn't the life he had grown up with, but it had felt real. For the first time, Nathan had felt like he was contributing to something that mattered.

And now, he wasn't sure which world he truly belonged to.

"Nate," a familiar voice called out from behind him.

He turned to see his best friend Lucas stepping out onto the rooftop. Lucas had been with him through everything—childhood, college, and the countless business ventures that had made them both wealthy beyond measure. But Lucas hadn't joined him on the streets. He hadn't been there for the bet.

Lucas approached, hands in his coat pockets. "Figured I'd find you up here."

Nathan smirked faintly. "You always know where to look."

Lucas stopped beside him, leaning on the railing. "You've been off since you got back. What's going on?"

Nathan hesitated. He hadn't spoken to anyone about what he was feeling—not Bryce, not Carter, and certainly not the board members or the media. But Lucas wasn't them. Lucas wasn't looking for a soundbite or a spin.

"It's hard to explain," Nathan said after a moment.

"Try me."

Nathan sighed. "It's like... I can't see things the same way anymore. All of this—" he gestured to the glittering skyline, "—it feels... hollow."

Lucas frowned. "Hollow? Nate, this is what we built. This is what you've worked your entire life for."

"I know," Nathan said. "But when I was out there—when I was at the shelter—everything felt different. It was hard, yes, but it was meaningful. It wasn't just about numbers on a screen or shareholder reports. It was about people. Real people. And now, I can't stop thinking about them."

Lucas was silent for a moment, his expression thoughtful. "So what are you saying? You're done with all this?"

"I don't know," Nathan admitted. "I just know that I can't keep living like none of it matters. That shelter—those people—they opened my eyes. I want to do something that makes a difference."

Lucas studied him, his gaze searching. "You've never talked like this before."

"I've never felt like this before," Nathan said.

Lucas nodded slowly, then looked out at the city. "You think Emily had something to do with it?"

Nathan stiffened at the mention of her name. "What do you mean?"

"I mean, you've mentioned her more than once. This social worker who runs the place. Sounds like she made an impression."

Nathan felt a pang in his chest. Emily had made an impression—more than an impression. She had shown him what it meant to care deeply, to fight tirelessly for others without expecting anything in return. Her strength, her compassion, her relentless drive to help—she was unlike anyone he had ever met.

But he had left. He had returned to his world of skyscrapers and boardrooms, leaving her to fight the shelter's battles without him.

"I don't know," Nathan said, his voice quiet. "Maybe she did. But this isn't about her. It's about what I saw, what I experienced. She just… helped me see it more clearly."

Lucas nodded again, then clapped a hand on Nathan's shoulder. "Well, whatever you decide to do, just know you don't have to figure it out alone. I've got your back."

Nathan offered a small smile. "Thanks, Lucas."

As Lucas left the rooftop, Nathan turned his gaze back to the city. The light had shifted, the sun dipping lower, painting the skyline in shades of orange and gold. He felt the weight of the world pulling him in two directions: the life he had always known and the one he had glimpsed during his time at the shelter.

Deep down, he knew he couldn't ignore what he had learned.

But finding the balance—finding a way to bridge these two worlds—was a challenge he wasn't sure he could overcome.

Fourteen

Proving His Intentions

Nathan sat in the backseat of the black sedan, watching as the buildings grew smaller and more weathered the further they drove from Sterling Tower. The streets became narrower, and the storefronts became more modest. It starkly contrasted the polished glass and steel world he had spent the last week re-assimilating into. He felt a pit of unease settle in his stomach, the familiar unease that had plagued him since his return.

As Nathan had instructed, his driver stopped a block away from Hope Haven. "You sure this is the right place, sir?" the driver asked, his brow furrowed as he looked at the surroundings.

"Yes," Nathan replied tersely. "I'll call when I need you to pick me up."

As the sedan pulled away, Nathan adjusted the collar of his coat and started down the street. The shelter's sign came into view, the chipped paint and faded lettering a sharp reminder of everything he'd been trying to forget. It had only been a week since he left, but it felt much longer.

When he pushed open the door, the familiar sounds and smells greeted him. The murmur of conversation, the clatter of dishes in the kitchen, the faint scent of disinfectant. He saw a few familiar faces glance his way, their expressions ranging from surprise to indifference. He was just another person passing through.

Emily wasn't in the main hall. A volunteer directed him to the office, where she was poring over a stack of papers. She looked up as he entered, her brow furrowing slightly.

"Nathan," she said, her tone carefully neutral. "I didn't expect to see you again."

"I had to come back," he said simply.

She leaned back in her chair, crossing her arms. "Why?"

Nathan hesitated. He hadn't prepared a speech, hadn't thought through what he was going to say. All he knew was that he couldn't stay away, couldn't go back to pretending that this place and these people didn't matter.

"I left because I thought I had to," he said finally. "But ever since I've been back in my old life, something's felt wrong. I can't stop thinking about this place, about you, about everything you do here. I don't want to just walk away."

Emily's expression didn't change, but he could see the flicker of something in her eyes. Uncertainty, maybe. Suspicion.

"I appreciate the sentiment," she said slowly. "But you left. You went back to your world. What's changed now?"

"I have," he said without hesitation. "I know it sounds... I don't know, cliché or whatever, but I'm not the same person who walked in here a month ago. You've shown me what it means to really care about something, to fight for something that matters. I don't want to lose that."

She studied him for a long moment, her gaze searching. Nathan felt his heart pound in the silence, waiting for her response. Finally, she stood and motioned for him to follow her.

He trailed her out of the office and down the hallway to a small storage room filled with boxes of canned goods, bags of rice, and other supplies. She stopped in the center of the room and turned to face him.

"If you're serious," she said, "then prove it. We've got families who need these supplies delivered today. Take one of the volunteers and go. No press, no cameras, no fanfare. Just you, helping because it needs to be done."

Nathan nodded. "Alright. Where are we going?"

He found himself on a quiet residential street, holding a heavy box of food supplies. The volunteer he was paired with—an older woman named Marcy—led the way to a small duplex that had seen better days. The paint was peeling, the front steps were cracked, and the mailbox leaned to one side.

Marcy knocked on the door, and after a moment, a young woman opened it. She looked tired, her dark hair pulled back into a messy bun. A small child peeked out from behind her, wide-eyed and curious.

"Hi, Maria," Marcy said with a warm smile. "We brought some food for you and the kids."

The woman's expression softened, and she stepped aside to let them in. Nathan followed Marcy into the modest living room, where two more children were sitting on the floor with coloring books. The furniture was sparse, the walls bare, but the home was clean and tidy.

Nathan set the box down on the kitchen table and started unpacking the items. As he worked, he listened to Maria and Marcy talk. Maria mentioned how she had lost her job a few months ago, how hard it had been to make ends meet, how much she appreciated the help from Hope Haven.

It wasn't just about the food, Nathan realized. It was about the connection, the sense of community. People like Maria weren't just surviving—they were trying to rebuild their lives. And the shelter was a lifeline.

When they finished unpacking, Maria thanked them repeatedly, her gratitude palpable. Nathan felt a lump in his throat as he looked at the children, their smiles shy but genuine. He knew he couldn't walk away from this—not again.

—-

Back at the shelter, Emily was waiting. She looked up as he entered, her expression unreadable. "How did it go?"

Nathan sat down across from her, his hands still dusty from handling the cardboard boxes. "I think I finally understand," he said quietly.

Emily tilted her head, waiting for him to continue.

"This isn't about making a grand gesture," he said. "It's not about proving something or winning a bet. It's about showing up. Doing the work. Not because you have to, but because it matters."

She studied him for a moment, then gave a small nod. "It does matter."

Nathan leaned forward, meeting her gaze. "I want to keep helping. Not just today, not just when it's convenient. I want to be a part of this. And I'll do whatever it takes to prove that I mean it."

Emily didn't say anything right away. She seemed to be weighing his words, deciding whether to trust him. Finally, she nodded again.

"Alright," she said. "If you're serious, then we'll see what you can do."

Nathan felt a flicker of relief, but he knew this was just the beginning. Proving himself to Emily—and to himself—wasn't something he could do with words alone. It would take time, effort, and commitment.

And he was ready to put in the work.

Fifteen

Grand Gesture

Nathan gripped the steering wheel of the battered delivery van, his knuckles white as he navigated the narrow, unfamiliar streets. Rain streaked the windshield, the rhythmic thrum of the wipers doing little to ease the tension coiled in his chest. He hadn't driven in months—hadn't needed to—but when Emily mentioned a critical delivery that couldn't wait until morning, he had volunteered without hesitation.

Now, as he squinted through the streaky glass at the dimly lit road ahead, he wondered if he had bitten off more than he could chew. The supplies in the back of the van—blankets, canned goods, toiletries—were urgently needed by a family who had just arrived at a temporary housing unit. If the storm worsened, the roads would flood, making it nearly impossible to reach them.

His phone buzzed in the cup holder. Glancing down, he saw Emily's name on the screen. He grabbed it quickly, tapping the speaker button.

"Yeah?" he said, his voice tight.

"Where are you?" Emily's voice crackled slightly through the speaker, her concern evident even over the static.

"I'm about five minutes out," Nathan replied. "What's the situation like on your end?"

"The shelter's fine, but the family's been calling. Their power's out, and they're worried the water's going to seep into the lower level. They've got three kids under six, Nathan. We need to get those supplies to them tonight."

"I'm on it," he assured her. "I'll be there soon."

"Just… be careful," Emily said. "The roads are getting worse."

"I'll call you when I get there," Nathan said, ending the call and gripping the wheel tighter. He could barely see ten feet in front of him now, the rain coming down in sheets. The van's old headlights barely cut through the darkness, and the tires splashed through growing puddles that threatened to pull the vehicle off course.

When he finally spotted the flickering porch light of the house he was looking for, relief washed over him. He pulled into the gravel driveway, wincing as the van jolted over a pothole.

Leaving the engine running, he grabbed the first box of supplies from the back and sprinted toward the front door.

It opened before he could knock. A woman stood in the doorway, her face pale, her dark hair damp from the humidity. She looked startled to see him, then immediately relieved.

"Thank God," she said. "You're from Hope Haven?"

"That's right," Nathan said, shifting the box in his arms. "I've got more in the van."

"Please, come in," the woman said, stepping aside. "We've been trying to keep the kids calm, but it's been rough."

Nathan followed her inside, the warm air of the house a stark contrast to the chill of the storm. The living room was sparsely furnished, with a few worn chairs and a secondhand sofa. Three small children peeked out from behind the couch, their wide eyes fixed on the stranger who had just entered.

He set the box down on the table, opening it to reveal cans of soup, cereal boxes, and bottles of water. "I'll grab the rest," he said, turning back toward the door.

The woman nodded, her voice trembling slightly. "Thank you so much. We didn't know what we were going to do."

Nathan made several more trips, hauling in blankets, flashlights, and more food. By the time he finished, his shirt was damp from the rain, his shoes muddy. The children had moved closer, their curiosity overcoming their shyness. One of them, a boy no older than five, reached out to touch one of the flashlights, his small hand brushing against Nathan's arm.

"What's your name?" the boy asked softly.

"Nate," he said with a smile, crouching down to his level. "What's yours?"

"Tommy," the boy said. "Are you like a superhero?"

Nathan blinked in surprise. "A superhero? Why would you think that?"

"'Cause you brought us stuff," Tommy said simply. "Superheroes help people."

Nathan felt a lump rise in his throat. "I'm just a guy trying to help out," he said gently. "But I think you're pretty brave. You've got to be a hero for your family too, okay?"

Tommy nodded solemnly. "Okay."

Nathan stood, brushing off his hands. The woman looked at him with a mixture of gratitude and exhaustion. "I don't know how to thank you," she said. "This means more than you know."

"Just take care of yourselves," Nathan said. "That's all the thanks I need."

He exchanged a few more words with the woman, making

sure she had a number to call if they needed more assistance. Then he stepped back out into the storm, the rain immediately soaking through his jacket again. As he climbed into the driver's seat and closed the door, he let out a shaky breath.

The drive back to Hope Haven felt longer, the rain still pounding against the windshield. Nathan replayed the encounter in his mind, the woman's relief, the children's curious eyes, the way Tommy had called him a superhero. He had never thought of himself as a hero—far from it. But tonight, he had seen firsthand what a difference a simple act of kindness could make.

When he finally pulled into the shelter's lot, Emily was waiting under the awning, her arms crossed, her hair slightly damp from the misty air. As Nathan stepped out of the van, she hurried over.

"Well?" she asked.

"They're okay," Nathan said. "They were scared, but they've got everything they need now."

Emily's shoulders relaxed, and she let out a small breath of relief. "Thank you, Nathan. I know that wasn't easy."

Nathan shook his head. "I'm just glad I could help."

She studied him for a moment, her expression softening. "You're doing more than helping. You're showing people that someone cares. That matters."

He met her gaze, his chest tightening. "It matters to me too."

The two of them stood there for a moment, the storm still raging around them. Nathan felt the weight of his old life pressing against the edges of his thoughts, but for once, it didn't feel like it was pulling him away. Instead, it reminded him of why he was here, why he couldn't walk away from this place and these people.

This wasn't just a gesture. This was who he was becoming.

Sixteen

Scandal Exposed

Nathan had never seen Emily like this before. She sat across from him in the shelter's modest office, her shoulders tense, her fingers tapping an uneven rhythm on the desk. The air between them was thick with the weight of unspoken words. Outside, the low murmur of voices in the main hall served as a constant reminder of the people who relied on Hope Haven's doors staying open. But at that moment, they both knew the shelter was in more danger than ever.

"They're cutting the funding," Emily said finally, her voice clipped.

"Cutting?" Nathan leaned forward, his brow furrowing. "What are you talking about? We don't even get city funding."

Emily exhaled sharply. "Exactly. We rely on private donations. But someone's been going around spreading lies about how we run things here—saying we're mishandling donations, that we're funneling money for personal gain."

Nathan's jaw tightened. "That's ridiculous. Everyone who works here barely makes enough to keep the lights on. Who's making these accusations?"

"I don't know," Emily admitted, her eyes dark. "But it's gaining traction. One of our largest donors called this morning to say they're pulling out until we clear up these so-called 'mismanagement' issues."

Nathan stood abruptly, pacing the small office. "Whoever's behind this knows what they're doing. They want to cripple the shelter. If we lose more donors—"

"We'll have to close," Emily finished, her voice breaking slightly.

Nathan stopped pacing, his hands on his hips. "No. We can't let that happen."

"And how do we stop it?" Emily asked, her voice rising with frustration. "We can barely keep up with the day-to-day operations, let alone launch a PR campaign to counter every baseless accusation being thrown around."

Nathan took a deep breath, forcing himself to stay calm. "We'll fight it. We'll find out who's behind this and prove they're lying. But we need to move fast."

Emily gave a short, humorless laugh. "Fast? Nathan, do you even know where to start?"

He hesitated for only a moment. "I might."

—-

Nathan hadn't been back to Sterling Tower since the day he left to help the family in the storm. Now, as he rode the elevator up to his office, his mind raced. His assistant, Rebecca, had agreed to meet him after hours. If anyone could help him track down the source of the rumors, it was her.

When the elevator doors opened, the familiar hum of the sleek office greeted him. Rebecca was already there, sitting at her desk, her laptop open. She glanced up as he approached, her expression curious but composed.

"Mr. Sterling," she said. "I wasn't expecting you so soon."

"Thanks for meeting me," Nathan said, his tone brisk. "I need you to look into something for me—discreetly."

Rebecca straightened, her sharp eyes narrowing slightly. "What's going on?"

"It's a long story," Nathan replied, "but someone's trying to destroy a nonprofit I'm involved with. They're spreading false information, and I need to find out who it is. Can you trace where the rumors are coming from?"

Rebecca nodded slowly. "I'll do my best. Do you have any leads to start with?"

Nathan shook his head. "Nothing concrete. But I've heard the same talking points popping up in multiple places—on social media, in email chains. It's almost like someone's feeding these stories to specific people."

Rebecca's fingers moved over the keyboard. "If there's a pattern, we'll find it."

—-

For the next hour, Nathan and Rebecca worked side by side, combing through articles, social media posts, and donor emails. At first, the trail seemed scattered and inconclusive. But then Rebecca's screen lit up with a new connection.

"Here," she said, pointing to the monitor. "Several of these articles and posts can be traced back to the same IP address."

Nathan leaned in. "Who's behind it?"

Rebecca clicked through another set of files. "It's an anonymous source, but the digital signature matches someone we've dealt with before—a consultant who specializes in... let's call it 'reputation management.'"

Nathan's stomach turned. "You're saying someone hired a PR firm to smear the shelter?"

Rebecca nodded grimly. "It looks that way. And from the patterns I'm seeing, this campaign was planned weeks in advance. Someone knew exactly how to plant these rumors and make them spread."

Nathan's mind reeled. The shelter's struggles, the timing of the accusations—everything pointed to a deliberate attempt to shut them down. But who would go to such lengths?

"Can you find out who hired them?" Nathan asked.

Rebecca hesitated. "It won't be easy. The firm they used is good at covering their tracks. But..." She glanced at Nathan. "You know, if anyone's got the resources to dig deeper, it's you."

—-

Back at Hope Haven, Nathan found Emily pacing in the main hall, her phone pressed to her ear. She was in the middle of what sounded like another tense conversation with a worried donor. When she saw him walk in, she quickly ended the call and hurried over.

"Did you find anything?" she asked.

Nathan nodded. "It's not a random rumor. Someone hired a professional consultant to spread this disinformation. It was planned weeks ago."

Emily's face hardened. "But who would do that? Who would want to hurt us?"

"I don't know yet," Nathan admitted. "But I have a lead. I'll need a day or two to confirm it."

"Every day we lose costs us more support," Emily said, her voice tight. "People are already leaving. Even the residents are worried we'll have to close the doors for good."

"We won't let that happen," Nathan said firmly. "I'll get to the bottom of this. I promise."

—-

Late that night, Nathan sat alone in the small office, the shelter quiet around him. His phone buzzed, and he saw a text from Rebecca.

Got something. Call me.

Nathan dialed immediately.

"I found a name," Rebecca said without preamble. "The firm was hired by someone named Richard Devlin. Does that ring any bells?"

Nathan frowned, the name familiar but distant. "Devlin… Devlin. Wait. Is that—?"

"Yes," Rebecca said. "He's the same developer who's been pushing to buy out the block where the shelter is located. If Hope Haven closes, he gets the property."

Nathan gripped the phone tightly. Of course. Devlin had been circling Hope Haven's location for years, waiting for the opportunity to turn it into luxury condos. When Emily had refused to sell, he must have decided to force her hand.

Nathan's pulse quickened. "So Devlin's trying to bankrupt the shelter by cutting off its funding. If we can prove that…"

Rebecca cut in, her voice firm. "If you can prove it, you'll stop him. But you need more than just a digital trail. You'll need hard evidence—documents, contracts, anything that shows he's behind the smear campaign."

Nathan nodded to himself. "Then that's what I'll get."

As he hung up, a surge of determination coursed through him. The shelter wasn't just a building to him anymore. It was a place that had given him purpose, shown him a new side of himself. He wouldn't let it be taken away. Not without a fight.

Seventeen

Love Rekindled

The door to Emily's office creaked open, and Nathan stepped inside, his footsteps hesitant. She was seated at her desk, head bowed as she sifted through another stack of papers. Her hair was pulled into a messy bun, strands falling loose around her face. Even in her exhaustion, she carried a quiet strength, a kind of determined grace that made Nathan's chest tighten every time he saw her.

She glanced up, and for a moment, her expression was unreadable. "Back again so soon?" she asked, her voice calm but cautious.

Nathan closed the door behind him, the quiet click sounding louder than it should have in the tense silence. "I wanted to talk," he said. "About everything."

Emily leaned back in her chair, folding her arms. "Everything is a pretty broad topic. Care to narrow it down?"

Nathan hesitated. He wasn't sure how to begin, how to put into words the tangled mess of emotions that had been building in him since he returned. He had always been good with words—convincing investors, negotiating deals—but this was different. This was personal.

"I've made a lot of mistakes," he started slowly. "And I know that walking away from here was one of the biggest."

Emily's gaze didn't waver. "Why did you come back, Nathan?"

"I thought I could just return to my old life," he admitted. "I thought I could forget everything I saw here, everything I felt. But I couldn't. Every day, I'd wake up and think about this place. About you."

Her eyes flickered with something he couldn't quite identify—hope, maybe, or doubt. "You thought about me?"

"I couldn't stop," he said softly. "Emily, you're the reason I came back. You showed me what it means to care about something bigger than myself. And I don't just mean the shelter. I mean you. The way you fight for these people, the way you put everything on the line without asking for anything in return… it's incredible. You're incredible."

Emily's arms relaxed slightly, her posture softening. But her voice was still guarded. "Nathan, you can't just say things like that and expect me to believe it. You walked away once. What's to say you won't do it again?"

Nathan took a step closer, his eyes locked on hers. "Because I'm not that person anymore. When I first came here, I was arrogant, selfish, and completely blind to the reality of the world outside my bubble. But you changed that. You changed me. And I want to prove it."

Her lips pressed into a thin line, as if she wanted to believe him but didn't know if she could. "How?"

"I'm staying," he said firmly. "Not just for a week, or a month, or until things get hard. I'm staying for as long as it takes. I'll be here, every day, working alongside you, helping keep this place running. And not because I feel guilty, or because of some bet. I'm doing it because I care. About the shelter. About the people who come here. About you."

Emily's eyes glistened, and she looked away briefly, as if gathering her thoughts. When she finally met his gaze again, her voice was quiet. "This isn't easy for me, Nathan. Letting people in, trusting them—it's hard. I've had too many people promise to help, only to leave when things got tough."

"I know," Nathan said. "And I don't expect you to trust me overnight. But I'll be here, proving myself, every day. Whatever it takes."

A long silence stretched between them, the weight of the moment pressing down on both of them. Then, finally, Emily stood and crossed the small room. She stopped in front of Nathan, her expression still wary, but her voice softer than before.

"I need to see it," she said. "I need to see that you mean what you're saying."

"You will," Nathan promised. "I'll show you."

For the first time in what felt like forever, a small smile tugged at the corners of her lips. "Alright," she said quietly. "Let's see what you've got."

Nathan's heart swelled with a mixture of relief and determination. He knew this was just the beginning. Winning back her trust would take time, effort, and unwavering commitment. But as he looked into her eyes, he knew one thing for certain: it would be worth it.

Eighteen

New Purpose

Nathan stood in the center of the main hall, his heart pounding as he looked out at the gathered crowd. The once quiet shelter was now buzzing with energy. Residents sat on folding chairs, their faces lined with curiosity and cautious hope. Volunteers lined the walls, whispering among themselves, their arms crossed as they watched. And at the front of the room, standing next to him, was Emily—calm, composed, and yet, he could tell, deeply uncertain.

He cleared his throat, gripping the edges of the worn wooden podium in front of him. The weight of what he was about to say bore down on him, but he knew it was the right thing to do. For weeks, he'd been working behind the scenes, pulling strings, making calls, putting together a plan that he hoped would not only save Hope Haven but transform it into something even more powerful. He hadn't told Emily yet—not the full scope of

New Purpose

it. But now, with everyone gathered here, he had no choice.

"Thank you all for coming," he began, his voice steady despite the swirl of nerves in his stomach. "I know many of you have questions about what's been happening recently. The rumors, the funding cuts, the uncertainty about whether this shelter can stay open. And I also know that these past few months have been hard—harder than anyone should have to endure."

A murmur rippled through the crowd, people nodding, their expressions somber. Nathan glanced at Emily, who gave him a slight, almost imperceptible nod. He took a breath and pressed on.

"But I'm here to tell you that it doesn't end here," Nathan said. "Hope Haven isn't just a building. It's not just a shelter. It's a lifeline. A community. A place where people can find not only the resources they need to survive but the support they need to rebuild their lives. And that's not something I'm willing to let disappear."

He paused, letting his words sink in. The room was silent now, all eyes fixed on him. Even Emily, who had been so guarded, was watching him closely, her brow furrowed in a mixture of concern and curiosity.

"Over the past few weeks, I've been working to secure funding that will keep Hope Haven running—not just for another month or two, but for years to come. And I'm happy to say that as of this morning, that funding is in place."

Gasps and murmurs broke out among the crowd. People exchanged glances, their faces lighting up with cautious hope. Nathan could feel the energy shift, the tension in the room easing slightly.

"It's not just about money," he continued. "We've also been in talks with local organizations, businesses, and individuals who want to contribute more than just donations. We're creating partnerships that will provide job training programs, educational workshops, and permanent housing initiatives. Hope Haven will be more than a shelter—it will be a foundation for long-term change."

Emily's hand moved to her chest, her lips parting in surprise. Nathan caught her gaze and saw something he hadn't seen before—pride. She wasn't just hearing empty promises. She was hearing the beginning of something real.

"This isn't just my project," Nathan said. "It's ours. I may have brought the resources, but the strength of this place comes from all of you. From Emily, who has dedicated her life to helping others. From the volunteers who show up every day, rain or shine. From the residents who keep going, no matter how hard it gets. Together, we can make sure that no one who walks through these doors feels alone."

The crowd erupted into applause. People were smiling, some even clapping each other on the back. The volunteers exchanged nods, their guarded skepticism melting away. Nathan felt a swell of emotion in his chest. He hadn't realized just how much he'd been holding his breath until now.

New Purpose

When the applause died down, Nathan stepped away from the podium, letting Emily take center stage. She looked at him for a moment, her eyes shimmering, before turning to the crowd.

"I don't know what to say," she began, her voice thick with emotion. "Except thank you. To everyone who's been here through the worst of it. To Nathan, for believing in us and fighting for us. And to all of you who make Hope Haven what it is."

Nathan stood off to the side, watching as Emily spoke from the heart, her words carrying the same quiet power that had drawn him to her from the start. He could see the weight lifting from her shoulders, the hope returning to her eyes. For the first time, he truly felt like he belonged here—not as an outsider trying to redeem himself, but as part of a team, a family.

As the crowd began to disperse, people approached Nathan and Emily to shake their hands, thank them, and offer their own pledges of support. Nathan felt a warmth in his chest that he hadn't felt in years—a sense of purpose, of connection. This wasn't about a bet anymore. It hadn't been for a long time. It was about doing what was right. It was about building something that would last.

When the last of the crowd filtered out, and the main hall grew quiet again, Emily turned to him, her eyes searching his face. "You didn't tell me you were working on all of this," she said, her voice soft.

Nathan smiled sheepishly. "I wanted it to be a surprise. I wasn't sure it would all come together until today."

Emily shook her head, a small smile tugging at her lips. "You're full of surprises, Nathan Sterling."

"Good surprises, I hope," he said, his tone light.

She didn't answer right away. Instead, she stepped closer, looking up at him with an expression that made his heart race. "You've done something amazing here," she said quietly. "And I think you're just getting started."

Nathan felt a lump rise in his throat. "We're just getting started," he corrected. "I couldn't have done this without you."

Emily's smile widened, and for the first time, Nathan felt like he was exactly where he was meant to be.

Nineteen

Final Test

~~~~~~~~~~~~~~~~~~~~~~~~~~~~~~

Nathan sat alone at a corner table in the shelter's dining hall, staring down at a cup of cold coffee he'd long since forgotten to drink. The shelter was quiet at this hour—most of the residents had gone to bed, and only a few volunteers remained, finishing their cleaning shifts in the kitchen. The only sound was the faint hum of fluorescent lights overhead.

But the stillness wasn't calming; it was suffocating. The sense of relief and hope that had filled the room during his announcement just days ago had been replaced by a nagging unease. No matter how much progress they'd made—securing funding, establishing partnerships, strengthening their programs—Nathan couldn't shake the feeling that something was still hanging over them, waiting to strike.

The truth came that night, not in the form of a sudden phone call or an ominous knock at the door, but through Emily herself. She found him there, still staring at his coffee, her face pale and drawn.

"Nathan," she said, and he could hear the tension in her voice before she even sat down.

He looked up, startled. "What is it? What's wrong?"

Emily slid into the chair across from him, her hands clasped tightly together. "I just got a call from our lawyer. The injunction was overturned."

Nathan frowned. "What? How?"

"I don't know all the details yet," Emily admitted, her voice low. "But it sounds like Devlin's team found a way to discredit the evidence we submitted. The court ruled that we don't have enough proof to justify blocking the eviction."

Nathan pushed his chair back, standing abruptly. "That's not possible. We had everything. Rebecca traced the smear campaign straight back to him. We had contracts, emails—"

"It wasn't enough," Emily said quietly. She looked up at him, her eyes tired. "The judge sided with them. They have more money, more resources, more influence. They played the system."

Nathan paced the room, his hands raking through his hair. "So what does this mean? Are we out of time?"

Emily nodded. "Unless we find some new evidence, or a way to appeal… it's over. We'll have to shut down the shelter."

The words hit him like a punch to the gut. Nathan stopped pacing and leaned against the wall, his shoulders slumping. He had fought so hard—harder than he ever had in his life. He had poured everything into saving Hope Haven, and now it felt like all of it was slipping through his fingers.

But even as despair threatened to overtake him, a small, stubborn voice in the back of his mind refused to let go.

"No," he said suddenly, straightening. "It's not over."

Emily gave him a tired look. "Nathan—"

"We're not giving up," he interrupted, his voice growing more determined. "If Devlin can use his influence to shut us down, then we'll use ours to fight back. I've spent my whole life learning how to beat people like him at their own game. If he wants a fight, I'll give him one."

Emily hesitated, uncertainty flickering in her eyes. "What are you saying?"

"I'm saying we go public," Nathan said. "We take this to the media, to social media, to anyone who'll listen. We show the world what Devlin is doing, how he's trying to shut down a shelter to line his own pockets. If we can't win in court, we'll win in the court of public opinion."

Emily's expression was cautious. "You really think that will work?"

"It's our best shot," Nathan said firmly. "I still have connections. I can get reporters to cover this. I can put together a team to manage the messaging. We'll turn the spotlight on Devlin and make him wish he'd never come near Hope Haven."

For a long moment, Emily said nothing. Then she nodded, her shoulders straightening. "Alright. Let's do it."

—-

The next few days were a whirlwind of activity. Nathan worked tirelessly, making phone calls, drafting statements, and coordinating with the small team of volunteers who were eager to help. Emily spent hours recording interviews, sharing stories of the shelter's impact on the community. Residents stepped forward to tell their own stories—of how Hope Haven had given them a second chance, a safe place, a reason to hope again.

The media campaign gained momentum quickly. Local news outlets picked up the story first, running headlines like, "Developer Seeks to Shut Down Lifesaving Shelter" and "Hope Haven Residents Fight Back Against Eviction." The story spread online, with hashtags like SaveHopeHaven and StopDevlin trending on social media.

But with every step forward, Devlin's team pushed back. New accusations surfaced, claiming the shelter wasn't as effective

Final Test

as it claimed. Paid commentators flooded online forums with disparaging comments, trying to discredit Emily and the staff. It was a relentless tug-of-war, and Nathan felt the pressure mounting with every passing day.

Then, on the eve of the final court deadline, Nathan received an anonymous email. The subject line read: "Evidence You Need".

He opened it cautiously, unsure if it was a trap or a genuine lead. The email contained a series of documents—internal memos from Devlin's company, emails between his legal team and the consultant who had orchestrated the smear campaign, and a financial report showing payments made to silence key witnesses.

Nathan's pulse quickened as he scanned the files. If these documents were real, they were exactly what they needed to prove Devlin's underhanded tactics.

He immediately called Emily, his voice trembling with a mix of excitement and urgency. "I think we have what we need. I think we can win."

—-

The next morning, armed with the new evidence, Nathan and Emily marched into the courtroom one last time. Their lawyer presented the documents, laying out a clear trail of corruption and deceit. The judge reviewed the evidence carefully, his expression growing more serious with each passing minute.

Devlin's legal team scrambled to respond, but the weight of the proof was undeniable. In the end, the judge issued a new ruling—one that invalidated the eviction order and put a halt to Devlin's plans.

Nathan sat back in his chair, letting out a breath he hadn't realized he'd been holding. Emily turned to him, a rare, genuine smile breaking through the tension.

"We did it," she whispered.

"No," Nathan said, his voice steady. "You did it. I just helped."

As they walked out of the courtroom, the crowd of reporters outside erupted into a frenzy. Cameras flashed, microphones were thrust forward, and voices called out for statements. Nathan ignored them all. He wasn't here for the spotlight.

Emily stepped closer, her voice low. "Thank you, Nathan. For everything."

He looked at her, his chest tightening. "I'd do it all over again if it meant saving this place."

She smiled, and for the first time since this fight began, Nathan felt a sense of peace. They had won. Hope Haven was safe. And while the battle had tested him in ways he never expected, it had also shown him who he truly was—and who he wanted to be.

Twenty

Happily Ever After

Nathan walked into Hope Haven's dining hall on a crisp autumn morning, carrying a tray of fresh bread he'd picked up on his way. The shelter was bustling, filled with chatter and laughter. After the storm of the past few months, the air felt lighter, brighter—hopeful.

He set the tray on the counter, nodding to a volunteer who was wiping down the tables. "Where's Emily?" he asked.

"Out back," the volunteer replied, motioning toward the kitchen door. "She's helping unload a delivery."

Nathan headed toward the back, pushing open the swinging door that led to the loading area. Emily was there, overseeing the drop-off of donated produce and supplies. She wore her usual combination of jeans, a flannel shirt, and her well-worn boots. Her hair was tied back, but a few strands had escaped, framing her face. She was laughing at something one of the delivery drivers had said, and the sound of it made Nathan's chest tighten in the best possible way.

As if sensing his presence, she turned and saw him standing there. Her smile shifted slightly, softening. "Hey," she said, stepping away from the truck. "You're here early."

"Thought I'd lend a hand," he said, nodding toward the boxes. "Need help?"

"Always," she said with a smirk, handing him a crate of apples. "How's it going out there?"

"Busy," Nathan replied, setting the crate down on the nearby table. "But a good kind of busy. The new volunteers are settling in, and the residents seem… happier."

Emily leaned against the table, crossing her arms. "It's amazing what a little stability can do."

"A little stability and a lot of hard work," Nathan corrected, his gaze meeting hers. "You've built something incredible here."

Her cheeks flushed faintly, and she looked away for a moment. "We built it together," she said softly.

He studied her face, remembering all the battles they'd fought—against the eviction, against the rumors, against the odds. They had come out stronger, and through it all, Nathan had realized something he hadn't been able to put into words before.

"I need to talk to you about something," he said, his tone serious.

Emily tilted her head, curiosity flickering in her eyes. "What's on your mind?"

Nathan hesitated, gathering his thoughts. "I've been thinking a lot about what comes next—what I want my life to look like now that we've gotten through the worst of this."

She nodded, waiting for him to continue.

"I used to think my purpose was making deals, building companies, growing my wealth," he said. "But that never really made me happy. It just kept me busy."

He paused, his chest tightening as he tried to find the right words. "When I came here—when I met you—I started to see things differently. I saw what it meant to fight for something that mattered. To give without expecting anything in return."

Emily's expression softened, and she stepped closer. "You've given a lot, Nathan. More than anyone could have asked."

"That's just it," he said, his voice low. "I don't want to stop. I want to keep building this with you. Not just the shelter, but… everything. I want to be a part of your life, Emily. If you'll let me."

Her eyes widened slightly, and for a moment, the world seemed to hold its breath. Then, a smile broke across her face—genuine, warm, and brighter than the morning sun. "You're already a part of my life, Nathan," she said. "I don't know what I would've done without you."

Relief flooded through him, and he took her hand in his, lacing his fingers with hers. "You're the reason I stayed," he said. "You're the reason I'm here now."

She squeezed his hand, her eyes shining. "And you're the reason I didn't give up. You're the reason we won."

They stood there for a moment, holding onto each other, the weight of everything they'd been through finally lifting. For the first time, Nathan felt completely at peace.

Emily broke the silence with a quiet laugh. "So… what now?"

"Now," Nathan said with a grin, "we keep doing what we've been doing. But maybe, this time, we let ourselves enjoy it a little more."

She laughed again, and he felt his chest swell. There was still work to do—there always would be—but they had found something rare and precious in the chaos. They had found each other.

And for Nathan, that was the real happily ever after.

www.ingramcontent.com/pod-product-compliance
Lightning Source LLC
LaVergne TN
LVHW011955070526
838202LV00054B/4928